Original title:
Magnetic

Copyright © 2024 Book Fairy Publishing
All rights reserved.

Editor: Theodor Taimla
Author: Melani Helimets
ISBN HARDBACK: 978-9916-756-78-2
ISBN PAPERBACK: 978-9916-756-79-9

Orbital Bond

In the cosmic dance we twirl,
Two celestial bodies sway,
Bound by forces unseen and pure,
Through night and brilliant day.

Gravity, the unseen chain,
Tethers us in endless flight,
Round and round, though paths may strain,
We harmonize in the light.

Eclipses cast their fleeting shade,
Yet never obscure our glow,
In our bond, all fears do fade,
Love immortal as we go.

Nebulas watch with ancient eyes,
As we traverse the starlit sea,
In silent space, where no sound flies,
We orbit; you and me.

Through the void we carve our mark,
Unseen, yet ever profound,
In our bond, no endless dark,
Only the universe's sound.

Pulsar Pulse

Beneath the night, a distant light
Its rhythm, sure, both calm and bright
A heartbeat of the cosmos wide
Whispers secrets stars confide

Mysteries tick within their time
Spinning cores in cosmic crime
Their pulses reach through voids immense
Touching hearts with hidden sense

Guiding ships through endless black
With a path light cannot track
A silent call for those who stray
Reminding them of Milky Way

Time's beacon in the dark abyss
Each second marked with ancient kiss
Where nothingness seems bleak and cold
Their songs of history softly told

Invisible Grip

An unseen hand, it shapes our fate
In shadows deep, it lies in wait
Pulled by strings we cannot see
Its power vast, its reach set free

Whispers carried on the breeze
Subtle shifts that none appease
Guiding steps we never chose
Life's silent hand in secret prose

Choices made with tug unseen
By forces felt but never seen
This grip that holds tight, yet so soft
Lifting dreams, or casting off

Fate's agent with an airy touch
So far away, and yet so much
Invisible, yet always near
It steers the soul, as if by mere

Nature's Tug

By riverbanks through rolling hills
Nature's force, it softly fills
With unseen threads that pull and weave
Binding life, the sense to cleave

A dance beneath the verdant shade
With every step, a bond is made
Grass beneath and skies above
Nature's tug, a gentle shove

From roots below to leaves on high
A network vast beneath the sky
A silent call to earth and tree
Nature's tug will set us free

The pull of tides, the sway of breeze
Through silent woods and ancient seas
In every beat, it pulses deep
Nature's tug, our souls to keep

No Escape

Cloaked in night, with shadows near
Walls unseen, yet felt so clear
No escape from life's tight grip
Bound by threads that twist and slip

In every breath, in every sigh
A chain unseen that binds us nigh
To destiny and fate's harsh game
In circles tight, we lay the same

No door to free us from this maze
Lost in endless, winding ways
With silent screams that no one hears
In tangled webs of hidden fears

Though escape might seem so near
In hearts it grows, this secret fear
Yet in its grip, we find our stay
For in its bounds, we find our way

Anchored Selves

In the quiet harbor, we reside,
Hearts anchored by the changing tide.
Roots entwined in silent depth,
Love's whisper through each breath.

In stillness, find the strength to be,
Amidst the vast and open sea.
Together in this sacred bind,
Anchored selves, forever kind.

Echoes of the days gone past,
Moments held, too dear to last.
Yet in our stead, we're standing tall,
Bound by memories we recall.

Waters may churn and skies may quake,
But our essence will never break.
For anchored deep within our soul,
Is a unity that makes us whole.

Twisted Fates

Twisted fates, in shadows lurk,
Paths unseen, where dreams unwork.
Threads of time, in tangles weave,
Mysteries that minds conceive.

Destinations far and near,
Marked by choices wrapped in fear.
Whispers of the ancients tell,
Of futures hidden, secrets dwell.

Complex dances, life's ballet,
Twisted fates in grand display.
Every step, a turn unknown,
In this theatre all alone.

Chance and fortune, hand in hand,
Map the course across the land.
What was will be and might have been,
In twisted fates, they find their kin.

Cosmic Gravitation

Midnight stars in vast array,
Cosmic tales they silently say.
Gravitational pull so grand,
Universe at love's command.

Planets dance in rhythmic grace,
Bound by forces none can trace.
Far and near, in scope they span,
Cosmic gravitation's plan.

Celestial bodies, all aligned,
Wander in a path divined.
Each attraction, endless might,
Drawn together in the night.

Mysteries of space unfold,
Whispered secrets, ages old.
In the dark, a force unseen,
Guides us through this cosmic dream.

Energetic Fusion

In the core where atoms fuse,
Energetic sparks break loose.
Power from a union bright,
Lights the world with endless light.

Fusion of the hearts we bear,
Energies beyond compare.
In each touch, a power grows,
Fueling fire the universe knows.

Electrons dance in fervent spin,
In this love where we begin.
Together, we ignite the night,
With a flame, eternally bright.

Synergy of souls as one,
Like the stars, we burn and run.
Energetic fusion's song,
In each other, we belong.

Destiny's Gravity

Upon the threads of time's embrace,
We weave a path, each step aligned.
Drawn by forces none can trace,
Our destinies, together, bind.

Through the voids of cosmic seas,
Our hearts converge, a silent call.
Gravity of fates decrees,
Together we shall rise, or fall.

In the dance of stars we found,
A pull that neither force denies.
Destiny's gravity profound,
In each other's gaze we rise.

Beneath the skies both vast and free,
Magnetic forces, unseen guide.
It is written; you and me,
In destiny's gravity, we abide.

Attraction Paradox

In the shadowed fields of wonder,
Where opposites attract their kin.
A paradox, a world asunder,
Truths emerge from deep within.

Tangled laws of cosmic measure,
Hearts defy what minds construe.
Finding pain and hidden pleasure,
In the path that leads to you.

Bound by rules of contradiction,
Souls ignite in frictioned grace.
Love, a wild benediction,
In the paradox, we trace.

Mysteries of intertwined fate,
Thought and passion, side by side.
An attraction none can estimate,
In paradox, let hearts collide.

Mysterious Pull

In the night, a call resounding,
Pulling hearts to realms unknown.
Mysteries eternally surrounding,
Bound by forces, we are shown.

Beneath the moon's ethereal light,
Whispers cross the silent glade.
Drawing souls to hidden sight,
In darkness, destinies are made.

An unseen hand that carves our course,
Guides our steps with gentle grace.
Mysterious pull, the secret force,
In its embrace, we find our place.

Beyond the reach of mortal ken,
A power subtle, yet profound.
Mysterious pull, again and again,
In its thrall, we're spellbound.

Universal Lure

In the vast expanse of night,
Stars will whisper ancient lore.
Drawing minds towards the light,
Of a universe to explore.

Wanderers on celestial trails,
Hear the siren call of stars.
Universal lure prevails,
Guiding what is near and far.

Galaxies beckon with a gleam,
Unseen forces, cosmic dance.
In the endless cosmic scheme,
We succumb to its romance.

The universe, a grand expanse,
Whispers secrets, pure and sure.
In its infinite expanse,
We are drawn by its allure.

Invisible Pull

Across the silent void we drift,
Unseen yet ever near,
A force that moves in shadows cast,
In whispers we adhere.

Through night and day it weaves its thread,
A bond none can deny,
Unbroken by the hands of time,
Our spirits intertwined.

A dance of stars within our grasp,
Yet still just out of reach,
This pull that binds, unseen, unfelt,
Its secrets left to teach.

Our hearts respond to what we can't,
Perceive with human eyes,
And so we move like planets drawn,
Through endless, starry skies.

Invisible, yet ever there,
This force that makes us whole,
An unseen hand that guides our way,
The pull upon our soul.

Bound by Polarity

We are the north and southern poles,
Opposing yet aligned,
Our energies through space and time,
Eternally entwined.

Electric currents surge and spark,
When opposites attract,
A force magnetic in its draw,
No science can detract.

In every ebb, in every flow,
A balance must be found,
For we are bound by polarity,
In circles round and round.

Yin and yang, the light and dark,
We shift yet stay as one,
Reflecting cosmic dichotomy,
Until our fates are done.

No need to fight the pull we feel,
Or question why it be,
For in this dance of opposites,
Exists our destiny.

Charged Affection

A current flows between our hearts,
Unseen but truly felt,
An energy that courses through,
A bond with which we're dealt.

Positive and negative,
In balance we reside,
Our charged affection pulls us close,
And won't be pushed aside.

The spark ignites with every touch,
A thunderstorm of love,
We're lightning bolts across the sky,
Below and high above.

Connected by this voltage pure,
No distance can disarm,
Through every pulse and every surge,
We stay each other's charm.

So let this charged affection grow,
As rivers to the sea,
For in this vast electric world,
It's you who powers me.

Cosmic Draw

Across the vast expanse of space,
Your presence calls to me,
A cosmic draw that pulls us both,
Though far as stars may be.

Through blackened voids and galaxies,
This force cannot be swayed,
An orbit set by fate's own hand,
That never shall degrade.

Nebulas and spiral arms,
Could never keep us far,
For in this dance of universe,
You are my guiding star.

Invisible yet powerful,
This gravity of hearts,
Brings us together time and time,
No matter where it starts.

So as we sail celestial seas,
And watch all worlds align,
Know that this cosmic draw we feel,
Is written by design.

Gravity Bond

In the cosmos' silent sweep,
Two bodies pull, a secret keep.
Invisible ties, so firm, so deep,
A celestial promise, in silent sleep.

Orbiting dance in voids so vast,
Eternal etchings, futures cast.
Their silent talk, a timeless lore,
Gravity's whisper, forevermore.

No chains can bind like unseen threads,
In space's realm, where love is spread.
A silent draw, the hearts respond,
Souls entwined in gravity bond.

Through dark and light, their paths entwine,
Unyielding force, a love divine.
A dance of stars in cosmic play,
Bound by force, night and day.

In vacuum's cold, they find their heat,
Two destinies, the puzzle's piece.
No force can part this sacred blend,
A gravity bond, no start, no end.

Celestial Drift

Lost in the wide, mysterious sea,
Stars and dreams in harmony.
Wandering hearts in cosmic shift,
Caught in gentle, celestial drift.

Nebula whispers, kisses of light,
On satin trails of infinite night.
Galaxies spin in a graceful twirl,
Secrets of time, in shadows unfurl.

Eons pass in silent grace,
Echoes of an endless chase.
Through nebulae fog, their paths adrift,
Journeying in this celestial drift.

Planets forge their silent vows,
Eclipses mark the time-bound hours.
Radiant beams through darkness rift,
Unified souls in celestial drift.

Universe's breath, a gentle sway,
In cosmic flow, they find their way.
Stars align, their fates uplift,
Bound forever in celestial drift.

Luminous Forces

In galaxies where silence dwells,
Luminous forces cast their spells.
Through night's dark veil, in whispers soar,
Lights that bind and spirits roar.

Each beam a tale of paths entwined,
In cosmic dance, no ties defined.
Radiant threads, through space they weave,
A tapestry of hopes believed.

Starlit whispers pierce the night,
Ancient secrets in their flight.
Shadows part to light's embrace,
A dance divine in endless space.

Each beacon shines a lover's plea,
In solitude of the cosmic sea.
Brilliant flares through dark forces rise,
Illuminating love in skies.

Guided by the star's soft gleam,
Near or far, they chase the dream.
Luminous forces draw them near,
In every spark, love's truth is clear.

Pulling Hearts

Across the void, where silence sways,
Two hearts pull in timeless ways.
Unseen hands that gently steer,
Souls united, ever near.

Orbiting round a central fire,
Tethered close by sheer desire.
Space's canvas, the artist's chart,
Sketches bonds that pull the heart.

Invisible lines through starlit mist,
Connections strong in the cosmic twist.
In every tilt, in every start,
Hearts entwined, pulling hearts.

From distant realms, their whispers found,
Gravity's song, their sought-out sound.
Tangled threads in a lover's art,
Bound together, pulling hearts.

Unyielding whispers, interlace,
Their love endures in time and space.
In infinite stretch, their journeys part,
Yet always near, pulling hearts.

Forced Together

In fields where magnets play,
Opposites attract their sway,
Pulled by forces unseen,
Two poles must convene.

Repelled by like desires,
Yet drawn by fervent fires,
An unseen tether tight,
In day, as in the night.

Two ends of different thought,
In dance, they've always fought,
Still, the dance persists,
Resistance cannot desist.

United, yet apart,
With every beat of heart,
Their bond, a paradox,
Unlocked by nature's locks.

Forced by fate's decree,
Together, eternally,
A duo forged by force,
On this magnetic course.

Polarized Embrace

Where ends of earth do meet,
In tension bittersweet,
The poles shall intertwine,
In arcs of force, divine.

Day gives way to night,
In nature's silent fight,
Opposing charges find,
A bond of undefined.

In every clash and pull,
The void can feel so full,
Embrace of different kind,
Yet unity, they find.

Through realms of space and time,
Their essence is a rhyme,
Magnetic fields align,
In patterns so sublime.

Polarized, they stand,
Upon this shifting land,
A gentle, fierce embrace,
In which they find their place.

Energetic Whispers

In whispers of the air,
A power, always there,
Nudge of the unseen,
In life's electric sheen.

Currents flow unseen,
In every space between,
A silent, constant hum,
That joins the world as one.

Through circuits, through the veins,
Energy never wanes,
A dance of charge and spark,
Illuminating dark.

Nature's lively shouts,
In every twist and out,
The pull, the push, the thrill,
In whispers calm, yet still.

Unheard, yet always near,
The pulse of life so clear,
A force in endless flight,
Through day and deepest night.

North and South

In compass held by hand,
The needle finds its stand,
North and south oppose,
Yet harmony, they know.

A world divided clear,
By poles, both far and near,
One guides to icy lands,
The other to the sands.

In balance they exist,
Each pull met with a twist,
The globe, a field so round,
Where opposites are found.

Seas and skies agree,
On paths for us to see,
Magnetism's call,
In north and south for all.

Together they define,
A unity, divine,
North and south as one,
Beneath the same, bright sun.

Tempest's Lure

Winds that whisper wild allure,
A dance with nature to endure,
Raindrops fall like silver beads,
In the storm, the heart recedes.

Thunder's call, a mighty roar,
Echoes through the skies once more,
Lightning weaves its fleeting thread,
Dressing night in glowing dread.

Oceans rise to meet the gale,
Waves that clash with fervent wail,
Stormy breath breaks through the night,
Filling souls with shivering fright.

Branches bend and leaves take flight,
Tamed no more by morning light,
Tempest beckons, free and pure,
Drawing all to its great lure.

In this chaos, hearts may find,
Peace within the restless mind,
As the storm begins to cease,
Leaving whispers of its peace.

Eclipsed by Force

Shadows stretch across the skies,
Veiling sun with dark disguise,
A cosmic dance of might displayed,
In silent power, unafraid.

Stars hide beneath the sable cloak,
Breathless, as the heavens spoke,
Softly trembling on the brink,
As night and day begin to link.

Moon ascends in sovereign stance,
Engaging in celestial dance,
Orbit binds them in embrace,
Eclipsing light in tender grace.

Moments pass in twilight's hold,
Ancient tales in whispers told,
Shadowed secrets come alive,
As darkness and the daylight strive.

Emerald dim and golden hue,
Merge together, born anew,
In the silence, truth revealed,
Hearts by force of wonder sealed.

Charged Fields

Beneath the sky of cobalt blue,
Fields of green with morning dew,
Electric pulses start to flow,
In the earth, a vibrant glow.

Energy through soil and air,
Currents strong and gardens fair,
Nature's heartbeat, steady, pure,
In this dance, life's true allure.

Blades of grass and petals too,
Vibrate gently, fresh and new,
Charged with life in every vein,
Flowing through the fertile plain.

Thunder heads rise in the east,
Announcing nature's greatest feast,
Lightning heralds skies vast yield,
Illuminating charged fields.

In the stillness of this place,
Nature's touch with gentle grace,
Feel the pulse beneath your hands,
Energized by Earth's commands.

Electric Entwines

Lights that flicker in the dark,
Ignite the night with bright remark,
Neon colors intertwined,
Electric dreams within our mind.

Cables twist and wires sing,
Silent hums through cities ring,
Currents chase through hidden lanes,
Binding all with unseen chains.

Voices whisper through the haze,
Woven in a digital maze,
Signals travel fast and clear,
Connecting hearts that once were near.

Screens that glow with soft embrace,
Cast their spell on every face,
Electric love, a modern quest,
In cyberspace, we find our rest.

Sparks connect each thought that flies,
Underneath electric skies,
Woven strands of light defines,
Our entwined electric minds.

Electric Symphony

Neon veins in the starry night,
Whispers of voltage, a glowing plight.
Currents buzz in rhythmic show,
Energy's dance, a vibrant flow.

Waves collide with a humming grace,
Through the air, they find their place.
Harmony in a circuit's hum,
Electric dreams in silence come.

Conductors weave their silent spell,
In each pulse, a story to tell.
Flickering lights, a bright caress,
Merging forces in soft finesse.

Splendor sparks in twilight's hold,
Charging spirits, brave and bold.
In this symphony, light sets free,
The boundless power, we all can see.

Electrons sing in whispered note,
In their path, our dreams they float.
Bound together, yet apart,
Electric symphony in each heart.

Aurora's Embrace

Silent dawn in northern skies,
A spectrum glows before our eyes.
Shimmering hues, a gentle grace,
Heaven's colors in close embrace.

Dancing lights in cold night air,
Whispers of cosmos here and there.
Twilight's brush in sweeping strokes,
Nature's art that softly evokes.

Veils of green with streaks of blue,
Lavender waltz with a golden hue.
Across the world, they cast their charm,
Aurora's embrace, so cool and calm.

Starry eyes watch with delight,
Mystic beauty in darkest night.
In every wave, a story told,
Timeless magic that never grows old.

Silent whispers in the sky, we trace,
In profound awe, we find our place.
For in each glance, we capture dreams,
Aurora's splendor in flowing streams.

Lines of Draw

Pencil strokes on paper's plane,
A world creating, not in vain.
Soft lines sketch a vivid scene,
In humble grey, in shades serene.

Charcoal whispers tales untold,
In each curve, new dreams unfold.
Contours blend with light and shade,
In artist's hand, such magic made.

Easel stands, a canvas white,
Invites the soul to take its flight.
Brushes dipped in colors bold,
Craft visions new, from stories old.

Sketches bloom like morning dew,
Fleeting moments capture true.
Lines of draw, an artist's kiss,
In every stroke, a world of bliss.

In this realm where visions grow,
From simple marks, vast wonders flow.
Lines of draw, a heartfelt trace,
Unveiling life in every space.

Charged Particles

In the void, they dance and play,
Invisible yet night and day.
Bound by forces, unseen strings,
Charged particles, the cosmos sings.

Electric charge with fields unseen,
Binding atoms in a silent sheen.
With every move, a world transpires,
Fueling stars, igniting fires.

Tiny sparks in grand design,
Through the cosmos, they intertwine.
In every breath and micro trace,
Charged particles find their place.

From solar winds to earthly ground,
In every beat, they can be found.
Unseen yet they move our fate,
In their dance, we celebrate.

Mysteries of the quantum world,
In their spin, the universe is twirled.
Charged particles in endless chase,
Crafting life in boundless space.

Binding Forces

In fields unseen, they intertwine,
Threads of fate, so finely spun,
Binding souls by course design,
Until their journeys meet as one.

Gravity's gentle whisper speaks,
More than matter, more than force,
Guiding hearts that humbly seek,
To stay their predestined course.

Atoms dance in cosmic play,
Connections form, they won't betray,
Entangled in the grand ballet,
They draw together every day.

Invisible, this sovereign tie,
Links us to a greater scheme,
Through unseen bonds, our spirits fly,
Merging in a shared dream.

The universe, with secret arts,
Molds each life and binds it tight,
Drawing love from distant parts,
In the silent, endless night.

Secret Magnetism

A pull that's felt but never seen,
A force that draws us ever near,
In shadows deep, where thoughts convene,
It whispers words we long to hear.

Each glance, a spark in twilight air,
Invisible, this tender thread,
Magnetism, secret and rare,
By silent signals, we are led.

The heart, a compass, ever true,
Finds paths unseen, yet clearly known,
Two spirits wed by heaven's glue,
Together, never left alone.

In quiet realms where dreams abide,
We feel the pull, so soft, so strong,
Guiding where our hearts confide,
To places where we both belong.

A dance of souls beneath the stars,
By secret force they're intertwined,
For love, not distance, sees no bars,
And in each other, peace they find.

Spinning Closer

In cycles wide, our paths align,
Spinning closer, hearts combine,
An orbit drawn by fate's design,
Two stars in perfect time.

The dance of worlds, a cosmic waltz,
We drift, we sway, with passion calls,
Our distance narrows without faults,
As love within us falls.

Each rotation brings us near,
A swirl of light, a growing gleam,
Your presence dissolves every fear,
In this celestial dream.

Our spirals merge, becoming one,
Entwined in heaven's grand display,
Two lives in love's dimension spun,
As night dissolves to day.

We twirl within the vast expanse,
An endless dance through time and space,
Together in this sweet romance,
In each other's strong embrace.

Tangled Fields

The fields we cross, so intertwined,
Threads of fate, in patterns wound,
In tangled paths our souls confined,
With destinies forever bound.

Each step we take, where lines converge,
Our stories blend, begin anew,
In tangled fields where dreams emerge,
Our shared horizon comes in view.

We navigate through webs unseen,
Intricate, these bonds of time,
Through every twist and turn between,
Together destined to climb.

The labyrinth of life's embrace,
Where love's true tether heals,
We find our place in time and space,
In these enchanted fields.

Our hearts, forever interlaced,
By forces strong, yet unfulfilled,
In love's true essence, we are traced,
Within these tangled fields.

Electrostatic Embrace

In the silent dance of unseen charge,
Protons and electrons play,
Opposite in form, they intermingle,
A force that holds the day.

From distant clouds they leap and bind,
In circuits, fields, and space,
A spark ignites, connections find,
An electrostatic embrace.

The whisper of a current born,
Through voids and wires it runs,
A meeting of electric storm,
In rays of countless suns.

Invisible, yet felt by all,
A pull, a push, they taste,
An endless drift where forces fall,
In electrostatic haste.

Thus drawn together, firm they cling,
In patterns formed by chance,
A figment of the cosmos' wing,
Their endless, silent dance.

Ironclad Affinity

In the furnace of the earth's deep core,
Metals meld and intertwine,
Forged in fires where tempests roar,
An iron heart divine.

With strength and will they stand as one,
An unbreakable decree,
Link by link, under the sun,
An ironclad affinity.

Oceans part and mountains bow,
To the might of forged embrace,
In every tool, in every plow,
The metal finds its place.

Bound by force, unyielding might,
Immutable and free,
In factories, in dawn's first light,
Lives iron's legacy.

Together as the ages turn,
Their saga speaks of strength,
In iron's song, we feel and learn,
A bond that grows in length.

Poles Apart

North to South and through the night,
A journey silent, long,
Opposite ends, both black and white,
In separation, strong.

Divide and conquer, yet they know,
A unity unwound,
Though poles apart, they ebb and flow,
In harmony profound.

Mountains tall and valleys deep,
The chasm of the soul,
Bridges built on dreams we keep,
To make our spirits whole.

Distances may forge the rift,
Two sides of earth and sky,
Yet in division, hearts may lift,
And to each other fly.

Opposing forces may repel,
But love's unyielding art,
Through space and time, it casts its spell,
Uniting poles apart.

Quantum Embrace

In realms unseen by mortal sight,
Where particles convene,
A dance unfolds in endless flight,
In spaces in between.

Quantum whispers, soft and rare,
A symphony of chance,
Entangled states beyond compare,
In physics' deepest trance.

An atom's kiss, a photon's glide,
A pair forever bound,
Through quantum seas, they side by side,
In harmony profound.

Beyond the grasp of time's own hand,
They flit, they twist, they race,
In worlds that we don't understand,
A quantum-like embrace.

So here within this micro play,
A boundless love does trace,
In quantum leaps, in night and day,
An endless warm embrace.

Fields of Connection

In the valleys of my mind,
Paths of dreams I seek to find,
Threads of you are laced through time,
In the whispers of the wind.

Our lives drawn in sketched arrays,
Days and nights in boundless haze,
Through the ether, voices raise,
Songs of old in endless praise.

Hands that touch, though distant lands,
In the spectrum of commands,
Hearts in rhythmic counterplans,
Feel the pulse through shifting sands.

Stars align in cosmic dance,
Fates converge by sheer romance,
In the chaos, there's a chance,
Fields where our connections prance.

Echoes of a shared intent,
Moments lost and moments spent,
Fields of green where souls have bent,
Together, our essence sent.

Invisible Thread

Weaving through dimensions, vast,
Past and future, shadows cast,
Binding souls that seem so fast,
Love transcends, its hold steadfast.

Colors in the void aplay,
Silent words we wish to say,
Through the dark, we'll find our way,
An invisible thread will stay.

Fingers stretch across the space,
Drawing close in hidden grace,
Ties that none could dare erase,
An invisible embrace.

Fated meetings, preordained,
Love that never could be feigned,
Hearts with whispers so ingrained,
With life's tapestry maintained.

Every pull, every turn,
Lessons learned from passions burn,
Invisible thread, we yearn,
In this dance, it's our return.

Suspended Between

Sky above and earth below,
In the middle, truths we sow,
Suspended, we ebb and flow,
Lives like rivers in a row.

Dreams on whispering winds aloft,
Moments rough and moments soft,
In the stillness, echoes waft,
Suspended, spirits faced and fought.

Stars that guide and shadows place,
In the space between, we trace,
Suspecting glimpses of your face,
Suspended in this infinite chase.

Time keeps us in a tender sway,
Night to night and day to day,
Suspended, thoughts in grand array,
Seeking paths we can't delay.

Questions birthed and answers found,
Hearts that beat in muted sound,
Suspended 'till we are unbound,
In this place, love forever crowned.

Irresistible Drift

Carried on a whisper's breeze,
Through the forests, past the trees,
Fates converge in gentle ease,
Buoyed by an endless tease.

Current strong, yet void of strain,
Flowing through life's wide domain,
In our hearts, it will remain,
Irresistible, though plain.

Stars and skies and winding ways,
Days and nights, and endless days,
We are drawn in subtle plays,
An irresistible craze.

Dreams unfurl like waves at sea,
On this drift, just you and me,
Bound together, pure and free,
In this journey, we agree.

Soul to soul, we intertwine,
Moments measured, love Divine,
In this drift, your hand in mine,
Irresistible, by design.

Attraction Veins

Through veins of yearning flows
A pulse of hidden dreams
Where magnetic fields trace paths
In love's electric streams

In whispers close and low
We synchronize our skies
Two stars aligned by fate
With spark in timeless eyes

The pull of undiscovered hearts
A force we can't deny
In gravity's soft bind
Our souls begin to fly

Fate's compass leads us true
Through currents wild and free
In vast attraction's seas
Together we will be

A dance of cosmic loss and gain
A universe reclaims
Bound by our attraction veins
Love itself remains

Singularity Knot

In the void where time does end
A knot of fate is tied
Singularity begins with us
On destiny's vast ride

Infinity in moments held
A spiral wound so tight
We twist the strands of time and space
Emerging from the night

Dimensions meld in heartbeats quick
A pattern born anew
Our lives enmeshed in cosmic threads
We weave a bond so true

Entropy becomes design
In chaos, we have found
A single knot of unity
In love, our souls are bound

Endless cycles come to rest
Within this boundless lot
Our essence in this universe
A singularity knot

Driftwood Hearts

Upon the waves of time we turned
Two hearts adrift in dreams
Each current brought us closer still
Where love's horizon gleams

Broken once by tempest force
Now healed by gentle waves
Our journey marked by salt and sand
In ocean's endless caves

Together we reclaim the shore
Where sea meets steadfast land
With driftwood hearts, we build anew
A sanctuary grand

Time's ebb and flow may never cease
Yet here we find our peace
Two kindred spirits intertwine
A bond that will not cease

Our driftwood hearts, resilient, strong
From ocean's depths, we rise
To navigate life's endless song
Beneath the boundless skies

Invisible Yoke

Bound by threads unseen but strong
In silence we are held
A tether of invisible course
Where depths of love are spelled

In tandem stride we move as one
Though distance may divide
An unseen yoke around us keeps
Our hearts forever tied

Through trials, storms, and darkest night
The bond remains unfrayed
This force unspoken guides us forth
In faith, our souls arrayed

Invisible yet ever there
A strength that cannot break
Our hearts are yoked in tender care
With every step we take

We carry love, our anchor sure
In life's uncharted sea
An unseen yoke that binds us pure
Till eternity is free

Unyielding Force

In shadows lie the dormant might,
Unyielding force in darkest night.
Beneath the waves of ceaseless time,
It waits, its power so sublime.

Through valleys deep, it carves its mark,
Embracing winds, igniting sparks.
Of granite hearts and iron wills,
It shapes the land with whispered thrills.

Resistance holds a fleeting grace,
In nature's arms, an endless chase.
Forward the force with silent cries,
A dance within the earth and skies.

No chains can bind this ancient power,
Nor mountains stand its final hour.
With every beat of vibrant core,
Life echoes through its endless roar.

Polarized Kiss

Two souls adrift on currents high,
In magnetic pull beneath the sky.
Their lips converge, the poles collide,
In polarized kiss where dreams reside.

A fusion sweet of light and dark,
Electric passion leaves its mark.
Opposites meet, the sparks do fly,
In twilight's breath, a lover's sigh.

The northern winds embrace the south,
In melting heat from mouth to mouth.
A worldly force draws hearts anew,
In shades of love's magnetic hue.

In perfect balance they remain,
Each kiss, a whisper in the rain.
A destiny, a pull defined,
Two souls as one, forever twined.

Electric Bondage

In shadows deep, the wires entwine,
Electric dreams in twisted line.
A spark ignites within the mesh,
Of supple flesh and steel enmesh.

A current flows through veins of silk,
Binding tight in hues of milk.
The pulse of life, a rhythm set,
In bondage sweet, two hearts are met.

The voltage high, a searing kiss,
Electric bondage in abyss.
An endless loop of love's embrace,
In circuits closed, they find their place.

With every surge, the passion grows,
In binding ties, the current flows.
A lover's trance in nether's weave,
In electric chains, they both believe.

Fields of Influence

In fields of green and golden light,
Where shadows dance in soft twilight.
Invisible the forces reign,
In whispers through the rolling plain.

A magnet's pull in unseen tracks,
Through hills and valleys, silent pacts.
Influence spans in unseen arcs,
Connecting hearts like glowing sparks.

Each blade of grass, a story told,
Of forces, strong and gentle, bold.
In fields beneath the endless sky,
The subtle bonds between them lie.

The sun and moon, their web of trance,
A cosmic dance in vast expanse.
In nature's breath, the fields align,
With currents pure, their paths entwine.

Irresistible Attraction

With eyes that shimmer through the night,
A pull that leaves no room for fight,
The stars align, the fates conspire,
To draw us close, with love's desire.

A glance, a touch, electric spark,
Two souls ignite, ignite the dark,
In silence speaks a hidden vow,
Forever's whisper, ever now.

The planets spin, the cosmos reel,
Two hearts as one, their truths reveal,
In gravity's embrace they fall,
To answer love's unyielding call.

An unseen force, yet felt so strong,
In harmonies that sing a song,
No science, reason can explain,
The magic in this sweet domain.

So here we stand, our paths entwined,
No other love could be more kind,
Irresistible, we dance, we sway,
To love's eternal, timeless play.

Fields of Force

In fields unseen, where forces lie,
Invisible to naked eye,
The earth herself, in silence speaks,
A pull so constant, steady peaks.

Magnets dance in quiet grace,
Invisible lines, their paths they trace,
From pole to pole, a gentle glide,
Fields of force, they never hide.

Each atom small, a world untold,
Electrons weave their tales of old,
In orbits round, their love they'd find,
In forces strong, eternally bind.

Nature's web of force and might,
In perfect dance, the dark and light,
From caverns deep to stars above,
All is held by bonds of love.

These fields of force, beyond the ken,
Of mortal eyes, of simple men,
Yet felt in every breath, and beat,
Where science and that magic meet.

Invisible Bonds

Not seen by eyes that seek the light,
But felt in hearts that take to flight,
Invisible, but oh so strong,
These bonds that hold us, where we belong.

Threads of silk, in twilight spun,
A tune of love, the quiet hum,
Binding us in ways unseen,
In moments soft, in spaces between.

An unseen chord, yet it maintains,
A sweet connection, gentle chains,
And though apart, we're never far,
These bonds unite us, as they are.

Distance fades, and time stands still,
For bonds like these, they bend at will,
In memories warm, in dreams so bright,
Invisible bonds, in dark, in light.

So hold me close, with heart and thought,
These bonds of love, were never bought,
In realms unknown, where spirits wend,
Invisible bonds, that never end.

Steel and Lodestone

A chunk of steel, so cold, so plain,
But lodestone's touch would never feign,
Together, they would always dance,
In strong embrace, a firm romance.

A magnet's pull, a force unseen,
In lines of flux, a path so keen,
Uniting them in fields divine,
A perfect match, a wondrous sign.

Through iron's heart, the magnet weaves,
In subtle ways, it never leaves,
A drawing close, a firm embrace,
A silent tale in every trace.

From polar ends, to center's core,
They find a bond, forever more,
No forge of man could e'er compare,
To nature's love, beyond the air.

Steel and lodestone, love so true,
In depths of earth, they softly grew,
A union that defies the years,
Stronger than all, void of fears.

Unified Currents

Under stars where dreams align,
Waves whisper secrets to the shore,
Echoes of times both vast, divine,
Hearts beat steady, yearning for more.

Moonlight dances on the sea's crest,
Bound by tides, souls interlace,
In silent depths, we find our rest,
Unified currents, an endless grace.

Songs of sirens, a soft caress,
Guiding through the night's expanse,
In this rhythm, we confess,
A symphony, a soulful dance.

Eternal rivers, paths entwined,
Flowing towards the horizon's glow,
In the currents, peace we find,
Together, through the ebb and flow.

Shifting Northward

Whispers of frost in the autumn air,
Maples blush with fervid hue,
Steps trace a path to lands most fair,
Shifting northward, skies anew.

Chill of winter softly creeps,
Blanketing fields in silence pure,
Beneath the stars, the stillness sleeps,
In its calm, our hearts secure.

Aurora dances, a vibrant feast,
Colors blend in cosmic play,
From southern climes, our souls released,
Shifting northward, where night meets day.

Mountains rise, their peaks aglow,
Breathing whispers, ancient, wise,
Guiding us through the drifting snow,
Embracing cold, where truth lies.

Sun's Embrace

Golden rays kiss the morning dew,
Waking fields in a soft embrace,
Every dawn feels fresh, anew,
Sun's warmth paints the world's face.

In the noon, shadows retreat,
Life hums a vibrant, joyous tune,
Underneath the sun's strong heat,
Hearts beat wild, like flowers in June.

As it sets, hues of amber blaze,
Horizons bathe in evening's glow,
In its light, we find our ways,
Guided by the sunset's show.

Night may come, with stars in tow,
Yet we await the break of day,
Knowing that the sun's bright flow,
Forever lights our chosen way.

Quantum Cling

In realms unseen, where particles dance,
Quantum fields with unseen strings,
Existence hums in a mystic trance,
Bound by the force of invisible clings.

Entangled states, in spaceless flight,
Through the void, connections ring,
Beyond the scope of mortal sight,
All of life, a quantum cling.

Atoms weave their hidden tale,
Spinning stories, vast, unique,
In every wave, potential dwells,
Truths we seek, are theirs to speak.

Parallel worlds in single breath,
Tied by threads of endless spring,
Love and life defy mere death,
Endless ties in quantum cling.

Silent Force

Winds that whisper, softly sing,
Mountains move, a quiet ring,
Nature's call is ever clear,
Strength is found when none can hear.

Through the hush, the seeds will rise,
Echoes dance as twilight flies,
Underneath the moonlit haze,
Power lies in secret ways.

Streams will carve a path so grand,
Silent waters shape the land,
Tidal whispers in the night,
Wielder of an ancient might.

Roots that stretch in silent loom,
Hidden might in forest's bloom,
Every leaf a testament,
To a silent force's gent.

In the stillness, truth is found,
Nature's strength without a sound,
Listen closely, heed its call,
Silent force, it moves us all.

Invisible Hands

Stitch the daylight to the dawn,
Crafting moments without brawn,
Guiding whispers, unseen crew,
Invisible hands weave through.

Beneath the stars, they gently guide,
In the shadows, they reside,
Fate's fine thread in quiet strands,
Woven by invisible hands.

Whispers in the morning dew,
Shaping worlds that we pursue,
Ghostly touch in every breeze,
Secrets held within the trees.

Tender grip on dreams we chase,
Subtle hints in time and space,
Threads of life that intertwine,
Held by hands that can't recline.

Destined paths by them designed,
In each moment, intertwined,
Feel their touch in life's expanse,
Gruel unseen, they take their stance.

Unseen Bonds

Ties that bind without a sight,
Threads of gold, soft as light,
Linked by whispers, hearts entwined,
Unseen bonds, yet defined.

In the silence, love prevails,
Mystic roots, no gale derails,
Friendship's string, with strength it holds,
Unseen bonds, enduring bold.

Through the distance, feelings flow,
Cords of trust beneath the snow,
Every heart, a rhythmic beat,
Life's unseen bonds, ever sweet.

Shadowed threads in moonlit dance,
Invisible, a true romance,
Binding souls through space and time,
Unseen bonds, so pure, so prime.

Feel the pull of hidden ties,
Glimpse the magic in our eyes,
Though invisible, they're strong,
Unseen bonds where hearts belong.

Mesmeric Allure

Gazing stars in twilight's bloom,
Captivated by the gloom,
Magic whispers in the air,
Mesmeric allure, standing there.

Moonlit paths that wind and wend,
Draw us close, with dreams to tend,
Night's soft glow, a siren's song,
Mesmeric allure, we belong.

In the silence, shadows play,
Guiding hearts to find their way,
Enchanting night, so pure, so true,
Mesmeric allure, drawing you.

Waves of night caress the shore,
Mystic dances, ever more,
Soft and gentle, pulling near,
Mesmeric allure, full of cheer.

Feel the magic in the air,
Lose yourself without a care,
In the depth of night so pure,
Mesmeric allure, always sure.

Irresistible Current

A river flows, an endless path
Through valley's deep, and mountain's wrath
Its whisper calls, a gentle plead
To join the dance, where journeys lead

In rhythmic sway, it pulls us near
Surrendering, we cast away fear
Unseen forces, currents guide
Two hearts adrift, on this wild ride

As sunlight glints on liquid gold
Stories of forever, they unfold
Each ripple holds a secret told
In waters deep, love's truth is bold

We follow this, the siren's tune
Beneath the stars, a lover's moon
The current's pull, our hearts will bind
To drift as one, in flow's design

Drawn Together

From distant shores, a yearning spark
Illuminates the shadowed dark
In twilight's glow, a silent call
Two wandering hearts begin to fall

Across the miles, a bridge is formed
Unseen by eyes, yet hearts are warmed
A pull so strong, it can't be denied
In mutual orbit, side by side

The tides of fate draw closer still
Through rocky paths and twisted hill
No force can break this sacred thread
A destiny by stars is led

In harmonic dance, the spirits twine
A melody both pure and fine
Each note a breath of whispered dreams
In unity, our love redeems

Radiant Union

In the dawn's embrace, we start to see
The union of hearts, a mystery
Two shadows merge, to form a light
A beacon in the darkest night

Our hands entwined, we face the day
Together strong, come what may
With every step, our spirits sing
In harmony, our love takes wing

As morning mist begins to lift
We cherish this, our cherished gift
The radiance of a love so true
A canvas painted, of me and you

Each sunrise new, our bond renews
With whispered vows, beneath the hues
Of gold and rose, our love is cast
A story told, forever fast

Orbits Align

In cosmic dance, the stars obey
A path ordained, where lovers play
Two orbs drawn close by gravity
Their fates entwined, in mystery

Around they spin, in endless flight
Through days and dreams, through darkest night
Each orbit brings them near again
A cycle vast, a love unchained

In silent skies, their hearts converse
In whispers soft, they claim the verse
Of timeless love, like starlit fires
Their orbits merge, in shared desires

Aligned at last, in perfect grace
A union sealed, in time and space
Two souls as one, forever bound
In cosmic dance, true love is found

Axis of Allure

In twilight's tender arms, we dance.
A symphony of stars, a mystic chance.
The night unfolds a lover's trance,
In silence's song, our hearts advance.

The moon above, a silver guide,
Through shadows where our secrets bide.
This axis turns, worlds coincide,
In love's sweet gravity, we glide.

Eyes whisper tales we've dared not speak,
Where passion's flames light each mystique.
As galaxies in azure leak,
Our souls in night's allure bespeak.

The dreams entwined in dark's duvet,
Two specters in a night's ballet.
Within this axis, time's delay,
Where love and stars forever stay.

We sway amid celestial's lure,
In heartbeats only night can cure.
This axis of allure, secure,
In love's eternal murmured purr.

Phantom Embrace

Beneath the veil of midnight's shade,
Where whispers of the past cascade.
A phantom's touch in dreams displayed,
An ethereal, transient serenade.

Her presence like a fleeting mist,
Enshrined in memories, bittersweet twist.
A ghostly kiss upon my wrist,
In phantom's arms, existence kissed.

Our hearts entwine through time's cruel march,
In shadows, love's requiem starch.
Each moment passed a buried arch,
An echo in the starlit larch.

In darkened halls our spirits waltz,
Through veils of time where silence halts.
A phantom's whisper, soft exalts,
In love's invisible, tender vaults.

Though dawn will break and dreams dispel,
Her phantom touch within will dwell.
In night's embrace, eternal spell,
Her ghostly love my heart will swell.

Field of Dreams

In fields of dreams where dawnlight beams,
Through misty morn, a fleeting gleams.
Imagination's endless seams,
We sow our hopes in thought's regimes.

The grasses sway in whispered lore,
Each blade a tale from days of yore.
Beneath the sky, our spirits soar,
To dreamland's gate, an open door.

The sun sprouts gold in morning's hue,
As dreams unfurl in skies so blue.
We wander paths where fantasies accrue,
In fields of dreams, our wishes grew.

Through time's ethereal expanse,
We waltz in daydreams, pure romance.
In fields, unhindered hearts enhance,
The realm of dreams where souls entranced.

Here visions bloom, untouched by scheme,
In moments where reality's deem.
Forever stilled in dreams supreme,
In fields of dreams, we dare to dream.

Lines of Fate

In fate's fine lines our lives entwined,
Through twists and turns our paths aligned.
In script unseen, our hearts consigned,
To dance where destiny defined.

Each stroke a step in life's ballet,
A pattern where our stories lay.
In fate's embrace we find our way,
To meet again in love's array.

Through trials and time, we're intertwined,
A tapestry in stars combined.
The fates conspired and so designed,
A love in threads of fate enshrined.

In every line a tale of old,
Through ink of heart, our fates unfold.
In destiny's embrace we're bold,
To cherish what our futures hold.

In lines of fate, our souls engage,
A timeless vow on life's grand stage.
Together through each turning page,
In love, our fates forever sage.

Attraction's Dance

In twilight's tender grip,
Two souls began to weave,
Their heartstrings start to slip,
Neither dared to leave.

Through whispers of the night,
And shadows soft and clear,
They danced beneath starlight,
Where silence drew them near.

Their movements, swift and slow,
A choreography divine,
In tandem they would flow,
No need for steps or sign.

As moonlight bathed their skin,
And stars sang lullabies,
They found new worlds within,
Reflected in each other's eyes.

When dawn began to break,
Their dance would never cease,
For love's own hand did make,
A melody of peace.

Pull of the Unknown

A horizon bare and wide,
Calls to the curious heart,
Adventure seeks its stride,
From journeys where we start.

The wind whispers its tale,
Of places yet unseen,
And through the sky's soft veil,
We chase a distant dream.

The road ahead unfolds,
With mystery in its wake,
Each step a story holds,
A chance our souls must take.

Unknown paths draw us near,
Their secrets to unveil,
For in each shadowed fear,
Lies tales where dreams prevail.

So with courage as our guide,
We wander to explore,
The pull we can't abide,
The unknown forevermore.

Invisible Currents

Beneath the surface, deep,
Where unseen forces glide,
Emotions silent creep,
In whispered waves they hide.

Our lives intertwined flow,
In currents fierce and mild,
In ways we may not know,
With grace so soft and wild.

Words left unspoken, stay,
Yet guide us through the night,
Invisible by day,
But felt in morning light.

Connections strong and pure,
Transcending time and space,
In love we find the cure,
A gentle, warm embrace.

Through streams of endless dreams,
Our spirits intertwine,
In currents' softest gleams,
Our hearts forever shine.

Gravity of Souls

In realms where spirits fly,
A magnetism pulls,
Beneath a starlit sky,
Bound by unseen tools.

Each soul, an orb of light,
In cosmic dance, they meet,
Orbit with sheer delight,
In rhythm, hearts compete.

This gravity profound,
No force on earth compares,
In love's great depths we're bound,
Released to sweep the airs.

Beyond the spatial seas,
Where timeless beauty roams,
Our spirits find their ease,
In love's celestial homes.

With every close embrace,
We feel the ancient call,
A gravity, in grace,
That holds us one and all.

Celestial Fields

Upon the heights where eagles soar,
Crystalline silence evermore,
Beneath the gleaming starry veil,
Celestial fields, we shall prevail.

Mystic winds through cosmic trees,
Whispers dance on astral seas,
Beyond the realm of time's embrace,
Eternal light and boundless space.

In living light and spectral hue,
Fragments of the universe accrue,
Galaxies like gardens grow,
In fields where endless wonders flow.

Nebulas weave a tapestry bright,
Planets born in the eternal night,
In every pulse, a cosmic beat,
Celestial fields, our hearts entreat.

Through endless time, our spirits rise,
Underneath those starry skies,
In harmony with the wild unknown,
Together, never more alone.

Attractive Forces

Invisible threads that bind us tight,
In the darkness, in the light,
From atom's heart to stars afar,
Attractive forces, who we are.

Through the void, connections blaze,
Energetic, through the haze,
Moments draw and moments flee,
Forces pull incessantly.

In every soul, a magnet lies,
Drawing forth through shared skies,
Seeker's heart and dreamer's quest,
Bound together, none oppressed.

Gravity's gentle, silent call,
Keeps embraces from the fall,
Life's unseen yet potent strands,
Interwoven through all lands.

From planet's core to lover's touch,
We feel the draw, intensely much,
In unseen bonds, our strength is pure,
Attractive forces, forever endure.

Orbital Allure

Round and round, the planets wheel,
Charmed by forces they conceal,
Dancing in a cosmic groove,
Orbital allure, they move.

Starlit paths their only guide,
In the dark, they effortlessly slide,
Elliptic whispers in the night,
A journey bound by unseen light.

Seasons turn and systems spin,
Gravity's pull from deep within,
In rhythmic sway, the stars endure,
Their dance, an endless allure.

In silent orbits, destinies lie,
Circles traced against the sky,
Each revolution marks the flow,
Of timeless beauty they bestow.

Majesty in every groove,
Eternal waltz, they softly prove,
Allured by forces strong yet pure,
In cosmic dance forever sure.

Invisible Strings

Threads unseen yet palpably strong,
Through every heart they weave along,
Binding souls in silent swing,
Invisible strings, a gentle cling.

Every motion, every breath,
Guided by love's silent depth,
Connections forged from ancient song,
In invisible strings, where we belong.

Tethered close through space and time,
Soulmates' rhythm, perfect rhyme,
In every joy and every tear,
Invisible strings pull near.

From cradle soft to grave entwined,
Unseen cords of hearts combined,
Life's symphony they gently bring,
Melody of invisible string.

Linger there, in bonds unseen,
In every thought, in every dream,
Beyond the veil where spirits sing,
Bound by those invisible strings.

Gravitational Clasp

In realms where dark and light entwine,
A dance unseen, yet truly fine.
Two bodies pulled in silent gasp,
In the gravitational clasp.

A force that bends, reshapes the night,
Invisible threads of nature's might.
With every orbit, paths redrawn,
Connections hold until the dawn.

No strings to tie, no chains to see,
But bound they are, perpetually.
The universe in fervent clasp,
In love's own perfect, silent rasp.

Millennia may come and pass,
Yet steadfast is that cosmic grasp.
A waltz of stars within the vast,
By gravity, all hearts amass.

Cosmos' Lover

A glance up to the midnight sky,
My soul begins its endless fly.
Amongst the gleaming, twinkling sea,
A cosmos' lover's heart is free.

Planets spin in rhythmic dance,
Star-lit lovers' timeless trance.
Whispers from the ancient past,
In cosmic dreams, my heart's recast.

Comets blaze their fiery trails,
Celestial love that never pales.
Eternal spark in darkened shroud,
Where loneliness is not allowed.

Galaxies in spiral arms,
Enfold me with their majestic charms.
Infinite space, yet not too far,
To hold the cosmos' lover's star.

Tracks of Attraction

Along the Milky Way we tread,
Invisible lines where hearts are led.
Magnetic fields unseen, yet deep,
In tracks of attraction, souls do weep.

Pull of planets, stars align,
Forces greater, most divine.
Electrons dance in quantum play,
In subtle ways, they mold the day.

Paths are drawn by unseen force,
In love's electrical, magnetic course.
No compass needed, hearts do find,
In charged embrace, they intertwine.

Amid the vast, uncharted night,
Electric sparks ignite delight.
In tracks of attraction, fate confined,
Destinies by force designed.

Drawn by the North Star

Distant beacon, steadfast light,
Guiding travelers through the night.
In heavens high, you shine afar,
Hearts are drawn by the North Star.

Navigators of the sea and land,
Trust your glow, your guiding hand.
Through tempests wild and calm repose,
A constant friend, your light bestows.

In darkest times, when hope seems gone,
Your shimmer keeps us pressing on.
A spark within the cosmic chart,
You lead the lost, you touch the heart.

Eternal in the sky you burn,
From you, we never wish to turn.
With guiding gleam, no matter far,
We're always drawn by the North Star.

Gravitational Dance

Beneath the cosmic, velvet sea,
Stars entwine in gravity's glee,
Planets waltz with silent grace,
Orbits locked in tight embrace.

Black holes spin, a shadow's gleam,
Bending time with eerie scheme,
Astral bodies sway and prance,
In eternal gravitational dance.

Galaxies in spiral spin,
Nebulae where stars begin,
Gravity's pull, a mystic trance,
Guiding all in cosmic dance.

Moons will rise and then they set,
Drawn by bonds they never met,
In the vast celestial expanse,
Life exists in this dance.

Among the stars and endless night,
Gravity holds with unseen might,
Threads of force, a cosmic lance,
Orchestrates the dance's cadence.

Unseen Connection

Between the words, the silent thread,
Tales untold and thoughts unsaid,
Hearts are bound by unseen ties,
In the hush where feeling lies.

Distance shrinks within the mind,
Messages in whispers find,
Though we stand on separate ground,
In this space, together bound.

Eyes that meet, a fleeting glance,
In that moment, souls enhance,
A web of throughs, unseen reflections,
We weave a silent connection.

Feel the pulse of shared emotions,
Flowing in like timeless oceans,
Across the void, a bridge erected,
In our bond, we're connected.

Words may fade in endless streams,
Yet our link in heart redeems,
In the silence, love's expression,
Lives our unseen connection.

Polar Harmony

North and south, the magnets pull,
Opposite yet never dull,
Forces clash, a balanced sway,
In their duality, they play.

Day and night, a mirrored stand,
Compliments across the land,
In their dance of dark and light,
Polar harmony takes flight.

Hot and cold in constant strive,
Heat departs and chills arrive,
In extremes they find their tune,
Nature's song under the moon.

Fire and water's endless chase,
Elements in each embrace,
Opposition finds resolve,
Balance helps the world evolve.

Through the contrast, unity,
Polar realms in symphony,
Life in balance, richly spun,
Harmony in two, as one.

Electromagnetic Whispers

Whispers ride on waves unseen,
Travelling where they've never been,
Electric currents through the air,
Send their messages everywhere.

Fields magnetic push and pull,
Invisible yet hearts are full,
In a dance of light and sound,
Electromagnetic whispers bound.

Through the ether, signals find,
Paths unseen to human kind,
Frequencies in endless quest,
Touching minds with their request.

Silent codes in dark and light,
Conversations through the night,
Waves that carry hopes and fears,
Crossing vast, eternal years.

Energy that binds us all,
Threads of light in cosmic hall,
Whispers in the night persist,
Electromagnetic trysts.

Pulling Strings

In the quiet of the night,
Shadows dance, pulling strings,
Whispers carried out of sight,
A marionette with hidden wings.

Dreams waltz across the stage,
Silhouettes of untold things,
Bound by fate, trapped in a cage,
Yet freedom in each pull it brings.

Hands unseen but ever true,
Guide us through twilight's rings,
In the darkness, piercing through,
Life unfolds as love sings.

Echoes of an old refrain,
Secrets that the moonlight brings,
In the mist, and through the pain,
Peace comes from pulling strings.

Lured by Forces

In the web of unseen threads,
We are lured by forces grand,
Whispered truths and borrowed dreads,
Guided by an unseen hand.

Rivers flowing ever free,
Drawn to oceans' warm embrace,
Stars above in vast decree,
Dictate both our time and space.

Every wave upon the shore,
Every gust that bends the trees,
All are parts that beg for more,
Falling deep into the seas.

Hearts entangled, paths aligned,
Pulled by destinies unknown,
In the tapestry defined,
We are never quite alone.

Galvanized Hearts

In the forge of life's intents,
Galvanized hearts beat as one,
Through the fire that never relents,
Melding in the midday sun.

Each strike brings a stronger bond,
Tempered by the trials faced,
Love grows deeper, and beyond,
Every hardship is embraced.

Steel and flame in wild embrace,
Hearts are molded by the heat,
In the spark, we find our place,
Purpose made beneath our feet.

Riveted by love's true call,
Joined together, never part,
Stronger we rise after each fall,
Forged within our galvanized heart.

Cosmic Cords

Threads unseen in cosmos wide,
Tie our fates and bind our souls,
Through the stars our paths collide,
In the dance of cosmic goals.

Every comet yet to burn,
Every planet in its course,
All connect on their own turn,
Tethered by a silent force.

Galaxies in their grand spin,
Whirling in a stellar maze,
Bonds that start and never thin,
Guided by the cosmic blaze.

Mysteries in realms afar,
Bound in constellations' lore,
We are what the cosmos are,
Linked by cords forever more.

Collective Pull

Atoms whirl in silent dance,
Orbit paths in cosmic chance,
Whispering stars, they glow and gleam,
Unified in boundless dream.

Gravities shift, align, and sway,
Tides of moons, night into day,
Mysterious forces interlace,
In the void, they find their place.

Galaxies woven, one by one,
Threads of light, and dark begun,
Each a story, shared and true,
In the vast, collective hue.

Pulling hearts, minds, and souls,
Towards a fate, a common goal,
Binding through the vast expanse,
In an eternal cosmic dance.

Stars align and meteors fall,
Echoes of a whispered call,
Unified by unseen strings,
In the universe, everything sings.

Irresistible Vortex

Spirals twist, and shadows bend,
Through the stars, this pull extends,
Deeper into depths unknown,
Where the seeds of fate are sown.

Whirling mists and gravity,
Draws the lost and sets them free,
In the dark, they find their light,
Within the vortex of the night.

Winds of fate and time converge,
In the dance where all emerge,
From the chaos, order springs,
As the cosmic chorus sings.

Drawn to depths, unseen yet near,
Through the swirling, timeless sphere,
Every soul, a path aligned,
To the heart of space and time.

Secrets held in ancient star,
Wisdom shared from near and far,
In this vortex, all unite,
In the endless, cosmic flight.

Charged Affinity

Electric skies, they pulse and hum,
Magnetic fields, they call, they come,
Through the ether, waves descend,
To the core where forces blend.

Atoms clash and bonds commence,
In a dance of arc and tense,
Energies with purpose keen,
Find their place in vast unseen.

Charged with purpose, forces play,
Spark of dawn to close of day,
Particles with paths entwined,
In the quantum, truth defined.

Waves of light and sound conspire,
Fuel the hearts of endless fire,
In the storm, a silent grace,
Charged affinity in the space.

Magnetic souls, they drift and draw,
To the place where none withdraw,
In this field, we find our peace,
As the currents never cease.

Pull of the North

Stars alight, the Northern arc,
Guides the way through night so stark,
Silent whispers of the poles,
Pulling ever-wandering souls.

Auroras dance, celestial flow,
Colors blend in mystic glow,
Nature's compass, strong, yet kind,
Guides the lost and leads the blind.

Through the cold and crystal air,
Every star a guiding flare,
From the frosty, ancient lore,
Pull of North forever more.

Voyagers of land and sea,
Trust the pull so faithfully,
To the haven where none stray,
By the North, they find their way.

Magnetic realms, unseen force,
Binds the drift and sets the course,
Ever true, yet mystery,
Pull of North in harmony.

Hidden Force

Beneath the stillness, currents flow,
A quiet force that none can see,
In shadows deep, where secrets grow,
Lies power hidden, wild and free.

In whispers soft, on night's embrace,
It dances, silent, endless night,
Unseen, it weaves in steady pace,
A tapestry of subtle might.

The mountains bow, the rivers yield,
To unseen hands that mold their path,
In quiet power, strength concealed,
It stirs beneath, devoid of wrath.

In every breath, in silent air,
This force moves swift, beyond all sight,
Its essence pure, beyond compare,
A hidden realm of boundless might.

Unity's Signal

From mountaintops, to oceans wide,
A signal calls, resounds, unites,
Where hearts and minds, in peace, abide,
In unity, our souls ignite.

A whisper on the morning breeze,
A call to rise, to stand as one,
In harmony, through strife and ease,
The signal's strength within begun.

No walls can bar, no seas can part,
The call that binds our hearts in grace,
In every soul, a kindred spark,
A beacon bright in darkest space.

Together, strong, we lift our voice,
As one, we answer to the call,
In unity, in shared rejoice,
United, we transcend them all.

Converging Paths

In forests dense, through fields so wide,
Our paths once lone, begin to fuse,
From distant shores, where hopes abide,
We walk as one, where dreams enthuse.

The crossroads met, where fates align,
In silence deep, our steps converge,
The trails we tread, in patterns fine,
In unity, our stories merge.

Each step a thread, in life's great loom,
Woven tight, our paths entwined,
A tapestry of shared perfume,
The scent of journeys, now combined.

Through tempest wild, and calm serene,
Our paths as one, forevermore,
In seeking truth, in spaces seen,
Together, finding what's in store.

Milton Keynes UK
Ingram Content Group UK Ltd.
UKHW050130270624
444593UK00005BA/60